ROUND and ROUND the GARDEN

And Other Hand Rhymes

illustrated by
Louise Comfort

WALKER BOOKS
AND SUBSIDIARIES
LONDON · BOSTON · SYDNEY · AUCKLAND

FOR RICHARD

The editor and publisher gratefully acknowledge permission
to reproduce the following copyright material:

"The Cherry Tree" from *Number Rhymes and Finger Plays* by Boyce and Bartlett
by permission of Financial Times Management Ltd, 123 Long Acre, London WC2E 9AN.

While every effort has been made to obtain permission, there may be cases in which we have failed to trace
a copyright holder, and we would like to apologize for any apparent negligence.

First published 1999 by Walker Books Ltd
87 Vauxhall Walk, London SE11 5HJ

This edition published 2004

2 4 6 8 10 9 7 5 3 1

Illustrations © 1999 Louise Comfort
This selection of poems © 1999 Walker Books

The right of Louise Comfort to be identified as illustrator of this work has been asserted
by her in accordance with the Copyright, Designs and Patents Act 1988

This book has been typeset in Cerigo Book

Printed in China

British Library Cataloguing in Publication Data:
a catalogue record for this book is available from the British Library

ISBN 1-84428-453-0

CONTENTS

MY LITTLE HOUSE

My little house won't stand up straight,
My little house has lost its gate,
My little house bends up and down,
My little house is the oldest one in town.
Here comes the wind;
It blows and blows again.
Down falls my little house.
Oh, what a shame!

My little house won't stand up straight,

My little house has lost its gate,

My little house bends up and down,
My little house is the oldest one in town.

Here comes the wind; It blows and blows again.

Down falls my little house. Oh, what a shame!

4

KNOCK AT THE DOOR

Knock at the door,
Pull the bell,
Lift the latch,
And walk in.

And walk in.

Lift the latch,

Pull the bell,

Knock at the door,

5

THE CATERPILLAR

A caterpillar crawled to the top of a tree.
"I think I'll take a nap," said he.
So, under a leaf he began to creep
To spin a cocoon; then he fell asleep.
All winter he slept in his cocoon bed,

A caterpillar crawled
to the top of a tree.

"I think I'll take
a nap," said he.

So, under a leaf
he began to creep
To spin a cocoon;

then he fell asleep.
All winter he slept
in his cocoon bed,
Till Spring came along
one day and said,

Till Spring came along one day and said,
"Wake up, wake up, little sleepyhead.
Wake up, it's time to get out of bed."
So, he opened his eyes that sunshiny day.
Lo! He was a butterfly – and flew away!

"Wake up, wake up,
little sleepyhead.
Wake up, it's time to
get out of bed."

So, he opened
his eyes that
sunshiny day.

Lo! He was
a butterfly –

and flew away!

Five little ducks that
I once knew,

Big ones, little ones,
skinny ones, too.

But the one little duck with the
Feather on his back,

All he could do was,
"Quack! Quack! Quack!"

Down to the river
they would go,
Waddling, waddling,
to and fro.

QUACK! QUACK! QUACK!

Five little ducks that I once knew,
Big ones, little ones, skinny ones, too.
But the one little duck with the
Feather on his back,
All he could do was, "Quack! Quack! Quack!"

Down to the river they would go,
Waddling, waddling, to and fro.
But the one little duck with the
Feather on his back,
All he could do was, "Quack! Quack! Quack!"

8

But the one little
duck with the
Feather on his back,

All he could do was,
"Quack! Quack! Quack!"

Up from the river
they would come.
Ho, ho, ho, ho,
hum, hum, hum.

But the one little duck with the
Feather on his back,

All he could do was,
"Quack! Quack! Quack!"

Up from the river they would come.
Ho, ho, ho, ho, hum, hum, hum.
But the one little duck with the
Feather on his back,
All he could do was, "Quack! Quack! Quack!"

9

LITTLE BUNNY

There was a little bunny who lived in the wood.
He wiggled his ears as a good bunny should.
He hopped by a squirrel.
He wiggled by a tree.
He hopped by a duck.
And he wiggled by me.
He stared at the squirrel.
He peeked round the tree.
He stared at the duck.
But he winked at me!

There was a
little bunny who
lived in the wood.

He wiggled
his ears as a good
bunny should.

He hopped by
a squirrel.

He wiggled by
a tree.

He hopped by
a duck.

And he wiggled
by me.

He stared at
the squirrel.

He peeked
round the tree.

He stared at
the duck.

But he winked
at me!

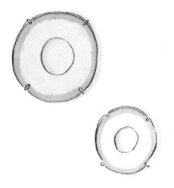

GRANDMA'S GLASSES

Here are Grandma's glasses,
And here is Grandma's hat,
And here's the way she folds her hands,
And puts them in her lap.

Here are Grandma's glasses,

And here is Grandma's hat,

And here's the way she folds her hands,

And puts them in her lap.

Here are Grandpa's glasses,
And here is Grandpa's hat,
And here's the way he folds his arms,
And takes a little nap.

Here are
Grandpa's
glasses,

And here is
Grandpa's hat,

And here's the
way he folds
his arms,

And takes a
little nap.

ROUND AND ROUND THE GARDEN

Round and round the garden,
Like a teddy bear;
One step, two step,
Tickle you under there!

**Round and round
the garden,
Like a teddy bear;**

One step, two step,

Tickle you under there!

14

THE SNAIL

Snail, snail, put out your horns,
And I'll give you bread and barley
corns.

and barley corns.

And I'll give you bread

put out your horns,

Snail, snail,

15

HERE ARE THE LADY'S KNIVES AND FORKS

Here are the lady's knives and forks,
Here's the lady's table,
Here's the lady's looking-glass,
And here's the baby's cradle.

Here are the lady's
knives and forks,

Here's the lady's
table,

Here's the lady's
looking-glass,

And here's the
baby's cradle.

16

TWO LITTLE EYES

Two little eyes to look around,
Two little ears to hear each sound;
One little nose to smell what's sweet,
One little mouth that likes to eat.

Two little eyes to look around,

Two little ears to hear each sound;

One little nose to smell what's sweet,

One little mouth that likes to eat.

17

THE SNOWMAN

Roll him and roll him until he is big.
Roll him until he is fat as a pig.
He has two eyes, and a hat on his head.
He'll stand there all night,
While we go to bed.

Roll him and roll him until he is big.

Roll him until he is fat as a pig.

He has two eyes,

and a hat on
his head.

He'll stand there
all night,

While we go
to bed.

19

HERE IS THE CHURCH

Here is the church,
And here's the steeple,
Open the doors,
And see all the people.
Here is the parson
Going upstairs,
And here's the parson
Saying his prayers.

Here is
the church,

And here's
the steeple,

Open the
doors,

And see all
the people.

Here is the parson
Going upstairs,

And here's the parson
Saying his prayers.

21

FIVE LITTLE KITTENS

Five little kittens
Sleeping on a chair.
One rolled off,
Leaving four there.

Four little kittens,
One climbed a tree
To look in a bird's nest.
Then there were three.

Three little kittens
Wondered what to do.
One saw a mouse.
Then there were two.

Two little kittens
Playing on a wall.
One little kitten
Chased a red ball.

One little kitten
With fur soft as silk,
Left all alone
To drink a dish of milk.

Five little kittens

**Four little kittens,
One climbed a tree**

**To look in a
bird's nest.**

**Two little kittens
Playing on a wall.**

**One little kitten
Chased a red ball.**

22

Sleeping on a chair.

One rolled off,

Leaving four there.

Then there were three.

Three little kittens Wondered what to do.

One saw a mouse.

Then there were two.

One little kitten

With fur soft as silk,

Left all alone

To drink a dish of milk.

23

THE FARM

Here sits Farmer Giles,
Here sit his two men,
Here sits the cockadoodle,
Here sits the hen,
Here sit the little chickens,
Here they run in,
Chin chopper,
Chin chopper,
Chin, chin, chin.

**Here sits
Farmer Giles,**

**Here sit his
two men,**

**Here sits the
cockadoodle,**

24

Here sits
the hen,

Here sit the
little chickens,

Here they
run in,

Chin chopper, Chin chopper,
Chin, chin, chin.

25

MOUSIE

Mousie comes a-creeping, creeping.
Mousie comes a-peeping, peeping.
Mousie said, "I'd like to stay,
But I haven't time today."
Mousie popped into his hole
And said, "Achoo!
I've caught a cold!"

Mousie comes
a-creeping, creeping.

Mousie comes
a-peeping, peeping.

Mousie said,
"I'd like to stay,

But I haven't
time today."

Mousie popped
into his hole

And said, "Achoo!
I've caught a cold!"

FOXY

Put your finger in Foxy's hole.
Foxy's not at home.
Foxy's out at the back door
A-picking at a bone.

**Put your finger
in Foxy's hole.**

**Foxy's not
at home.**

**Foxy's out at
the back door**

**A-picking
at a bone.**

THE CHERRY TREE

Once I found a cherry stone,
I put it in the ground,
And when I came to look at it,
A tiny shoot I found.

Once I found a
cherry stone,

I put it in
the ground,

And when I came
to look at it,

A tiny shoot
I found.

The shoot grew up and up each day,
And soon became a tree.
I picked the rosy cherries then,
And ate them for my tea.

The shoot grew up and up each day,

And soon became a tree.

I picked the rosy cherries then,

And ate them for my tea.

29

THE GOLDEN BOAT

This is the boat, the golden boat,
That sails on the silver sea,
And these are the oars of ivory white,
That lift and dip, that lift and dip.
Here are the ten little fairy men

**This is the boat,
the golden boat,**

**That sails on
the silver sea,**

**And these are the
oars of ivory white**

**That lift and dip,
that lift and dip.**

**Here are the ten
little fairy men**

Running along, running along,
To take the oars of ivory white
That lift and dip, that lift and dip,
That move the boat, the golden boat,
Over the silver sea.

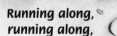

Running along,
running along,

To take the oars
of ivory white

That lift and dip,
that lift and dip,

That move the boat,
the golden boat,

Over the
silver sea.

PAT-A-CAKE

Pat-a-cake, pat-a-cake, baker's man,
Bake me a cake as fast as you can.
Pat it and prick it and mark it with B,
And put it in the oven for Baby and me.

Pat it

and prick it

and mark
it with B,

Pat-a-cake, pat-a-cake,
baker's man,
Bake me a cake
as fast as you can.

And put it
in the oven
for Baby
and me.